Love & Courage

S.L. Ritz

poems

| Rockville Publishing |

S.L. Ritz/Rockville Publishing
www.staceyritzbooks.com

Book Layout © 2020 ASEL Designs

Love & Courage/ S.L Ritz. -- 1st ed.
ISBN 978-1951523-152

Inspired by love, hope, and courage. Impassioned storyteller. Writer of books and poetry. Nature lover. Animal advocate. Lover of words. Captivated photographer. Believer in karma.

Written in the style of contemporary free verse, S.L. Ritz demonstrates the immense power of words and their ability to heal, connect, and unite. She possesses a keen knack for tapping into authentic human emotions.

A multi-award-winning writer and bestselling author, Ritz is a proud alumna of The Op Ed Project's *Write to Change the World*. Her books have been published in more than a dozen countries, including Canada, England, Germany, Japan, Switzerland, Republic of South Africa, Belgium, India, Oman, Thailand, Malaysia, New Zealand, Brazil, Australia, and more.

Learn more at **staceyritzbooks.com/poetry**

Note: Selected prose in *Love & Courage* are derived directly from Ritz's fiction novels. She writes fiction as *Stacey Ritz*. Find her works of fiction at **staceyritzbooks.com** or anywhere books are sold.

FORWARD

Words are powerful. They have the ability to heal. To harm. To unite. To divide. To comfort. To empower. To evoke change. To inform. To inspire. To connect. And to create endless magic.

The words shared with you in *Love & Courage* are poems written in the style of contemporary free verse. They are relatable words that reach for the hearts of readers around the globe.

This book is divided into three sections. First: *Love & Hope*. Second: *Heartbreak*. And third: *Courage & Resilience*. My hope is that the words contained within this book will inspire you to heal, connect, and grow, and to do all of the wonderful things that make you uniquely you.

We need more love and hope in this world. And it is my wish that the following words can help in some small way.

LOVE & HOPE

Our love is different

    I knew it from the start.

    For us

    there has always been

    a burning spark.

You told me I'd never have

nice *things* like you

if I married the boy

who came to you.

I told you I'd never have worry, like you

over *things* that meant so much to you.

The great blue heron

flies above us, once again

whispering silent encouragements

to nourish our souls.

When my fingers intertwine
with yours
I know
I am HOME.

The way the morning light casts itself upon you,
dappling your face in spheres of sunlight,
makes me believe the earth is singing for the love we
share between us.

My bare feet
cradled in yours
is all I need
to keep the demons away
a little longer.

Dreams of endless days
    at the ocean
with you
    keep me fully alive.

Forgiveness

in the face of everything

will keep us

WHOLE.

Whisper in my ear

and tell me

everything you know

of true love.

Long walks
on rainy days
always remind me
of who we are
and where we want to go.

In endless laughter
they sat
and pushed the bad away
waiting for the chance
to start over
with a bright new day.

"Just take my hand," he said.
"And I'll lead the way."
I shook my head
and answered
"I can't."
"Intertwine your fingers
in mine," I said.
"And instead, walk by my side."

I see you linger
   from across the room.
        Several years it has been,
            both facing issues of our own now
            that never should have been.
A slight flicker of your smile
   brings me back to a time
      when we thought we had it all.
         So many years gone by...

It isn't a competition.
　　It never was.
That's not love.
　　That's what a lack of it does.

You tried to reach me
from the other side of
nowhere,
thinking we had
D-I-S-T-A-N-C-E to spare.

Love is like an **invisible string**

between two people.

Always there

no matter the **distance**

or **circumstance**.

Push. Pull.

Pull. Push.

We seesaw

back and forth.

The ravens

watch over us

hoping

one day

we'll find the balance

that has always been

possible.

Please do one thing,
in the name of love:
Be brave enough to be **vulnerable** with me.
Be **courageous** enough to be exactly who you are.

One thread
you tugged on
and I became
unraveled.
Completely unraveled.

Love isn't cruel,
it is unconditional.
Love isn't pain,
it is healing.
Love isn't fear,
it is comfort.
Love isn't competition,
it is partnership.
Love is trust,
loyalty,
honesty.
It is
kindness
and compassion.
It is endless.
It is limitless.
Love isn't a sometimes thing,
it is an *always and forever thing.*
The truth is,
love is everything.

Love and other magical things
    surround us all of the time.
It is up to each of us
    to open our eyes,
to see the world for what it is
    instead of what we think we want.
It is up to us
    to see the gifts that Mother Earth
brings forth
    one day after the next.
The warmth of the sun on our skin.
    Nourishment growing from seeds.
It is up to us to see that we
    are loved.

No matter

what

they say,

I knew it all along,

it should've been this way.

We were madly in love,
always with our hands finding their way to each
other's.
Always laughing and carefree.
We were dreaming of our future together while
building it one brick at a time,
side by side.

I'm either the biggest fool
to have ever lived
or
the luckiest person
on the planet.
Or maybe,
I'm a bit of both.
Either way,
love is a risk I'm willing to take.

We kissed, both feeling the release of something that had been pent up for much too long. Both feeling that whatever existed between us was right and real. And both completely certain the feeling would last a lifetime.

I stare up at the stars...I stare at each one wishing I could lasso it and bring it to myself, stealing just a little piece of its hopefulness.

He sent me off with a kiss to end all kisses.

We were just kids.
We hardly knew each other
when you asked for a future.
I swiftly said *Yes*
as I looked at your soul.
Together I could see us growing old.
Against mountains of odds
we're still hand in hand,
both still saying *Yes* to the adventure.
We're no longer kids
but I still feel your soul.
Together we continue marching forward
building on memories, both new and old.

The value of being truly seen and heard by a loved one is priceless.

It's not the rush that makes it love.

It's the way you look at me.

It's not the Likes that come our way,
   and it's not the witty banter that gets pushed back
   and forth.

It's in the way you let me be.

It's not because we've read the same books.
   And it's not, as some say, because of our looks.

It's in the way you hold my heart.

It's not because you make me blush
   and it's not because you make a fuss.

It's because I feel I've known you forever.

It's not the way your breath tickles my nose
   and it's not because you massage my toes.

It's in the way you're truly you.
And in the way we're us.
   That's what makes it love.

It wasn't about the material things. It was about the invisible thread that existed between them. That's what meant the world to her.

I allow my mind to swim in the details of his every touch, his every look. The memory of today is still fresh on my lips and I let it all replay in my mind as if I have hit the rewind button on my favorite movie.
I can still feel his fingers on my skin. I can still feel the tickle of his breath on my neck…
I can't let him out of my mind. I can't let go of the feeling of wanting him and being wanted.

If you find someone you love and they love you back, if you make each other better people when you're together, if you are truly happy, **hang on tight.** The world will try to tear you apart because you have what they want. Don't let anything destroy the one thing that truly matters. Be happy. Be the best version of you and inspire the very best in your partner. If you're in love, that part will come naturally. **True love can only lead to a life well lived.**

Love is what exists between us.
    What makes it ours
is what we choose to do next.
    We can't hold it.
We can't capture it.
    But we can move toward it.

Accept the love you deserve,
no less.
And love, always,
with an open heart.

His eyes cut to my core and sent a million butterflies fluttering in my stomach. I love it. *I love him* and I wouldn't change this moment for anything in the world.

True love is when you find the person that makes you shine from the inside out. True love is when you bring out the best version of each other...True love is when you can make each other laugh in the middle of an argument. It's when being together makes you happier than being apart.

He placed his hand bashfully on my leg and I placed my hand on top of his to let him know that I wanted him there. We whispered nothing and everything into each other's ears.

What more do you need than love?

With him, I only have to be and by being me,
I am enough.

Love empowers us to do things we never thought
we'd find the **courage** to do.

It doesn't take much to make a happy life. What
makes a happy life, she realized, is spending it
with someone you love.

1917

If I could reach my hand across time
    to a century ago,
I would take your palm in mine
    and tell you all that I know.
Instead, you have reached your age spotted hand
    and placed it kindly in mine.
A quiet reminder of
    a million women who have come before me,
    providing countless privileges
    we so often don't see.
A simple gesture you've made
    as you lay your hand softly in mine.
A silent whisper,
    like a summer breeze,
    reminding me of the hands of time.
With one small gesture,
    you've done something I've dreamed of doing.
Some may see you as weak and fading,
    but I see your soul and you've done something
    amazing.
You've reached your hand across time as you've
    placed it in mine.

DIFFERENT GENERATIONS

We sat together
   smiling,
   just the two of us.
And despite the crowd that was swirling around,
   despite how difficult it was for you to find your
   voice, you found the strength to say,
      "Keep doing what you're doing."
After that, companionable silence followed.
Together we sat
   each looking and smiling,
      holding hands,
      old and young,
      forever united.

The **passion** between them was **strong**. Theirs was a
love that was **real** and **genuine**. A love that
tethered them both together by an invisible string,
reminding them that no matter how difficult
things could be in life, they were **lucky** to have
each other.

*I sleep best when her arm is wrapped around my
waist, reminding me that despite a million odds,
we always find our way back to each other.*

I pulled his body up against my own, pressing myself
against him, wishing I could transfer all of my love
and feelings to him by osmosis, if only I could
figure out how.

We have what matters most; **we have each other.**

He found love.
And love changed everything.

Although it went unspoken, they both knew this invisible thing that existed between them was anything but ordinary.

Right now she wanted to keep kissing the man who made her feel what no one else ever had.

He had never been more certain that love consisted of some kind of magic.

It is as simple as this:

connection and love

need to be nurtured.

THE END.

You can have all of the money in the world in your bank account, but if you don't have connection and love in your life, you are likely among the poorest of souls.

*Our relationship
has always felt as if it's
a conduit for magic.*

It's amazing what wonders
one true connection
can do for the soul.

Marriages
are such fragile things...
fueled solely by trust.

She knew right then and there that she loved him.

How can love ever be flawless and perfect when we ourselves are not? We are all perfectly imperfect, therefore, it only makes sense that real, genuine love is the same. *Perfectly imperfect.* It mirrors the two souls from which it's created. Love is merely a reflection of the magic that exists between two connected souls. Love is not just anything. It's everything. Love is all there really is. *For, without love, what else matters*?

I peered into the window
   and saw what we might be.
I saw both of us laughing
   and our carefree little ones
   running with glee.
I saw roses and blueberries
   growing in our garden.
I saw dancing and twirling
   and family meals around the table.
I saw tears coupled with exhaustion
   and tears coupled with elation.
I saw growth and joy
   and sadness and pain.
But most of all
   I saw you and me
   growing endless flowers in the rain.

You hold my hand at night
whenever I wake from a nightmare.
You say, "*Boo!*" when I have the hiccups,
so they'll go away.
You are, always and forever,
the love of my life.

They had the kind of love where,
in addition to an unquestionable passion,
they were bonded by an ethereal connection.
They often read books together,
feet intertwined
as they propped themselves up
on opposite sides of the same couch,
regularly reciting favorite prose
out loud to one another,
eyes glimmering,
hearts soaring.

TWO TREES
You loved me when I didn't love myself.
And I loved you when you needed help.
Like two emerging trees, side by side,
we let our branches intertwine.
Our love grew despite our wounds and fears
and we also grew throughout the years.

Our branches became a jumbled mess
while our trunks each expanded in mass.
Our roots grew deeper
and we reached for the sun.
When times were difficult
we leaned upon one.

Stronger we grew, day after day,
still side by side
making our own way.
Many have tried to chop us down
while others have laughed at the way we grew.

But you and I,
we always knew
that what we have is meant to be.
Side by side we're stronger,
you and me.
Despite their jabs and mocking laughs,

we continue to grow.
We never constructed our lives for a show.
There's happiness in being who we're meant to be.
We stand on our own, two ever-growing trees,
with branches intertwined, promising each other,
"I'll love you 'til the end of time."

When the one you love
    looks at you and whispers
    all the little things your soul longs to hear;
    how beautiful you are,
    how your laugh is infectious,
    and even how he misses you
    when you're in the other room...
    When the one you love looks at you and whispers
    through smiles and through kisses,
    the heart flutters with delight
    singing tunes and melodies
    night after night.

Sometimes I think the stars that sparkle above us in the black night sky are actually little holes from Heaven – little windows that remind us that our loved ones who have passed are still watching over us. They twinkle so we'll look up – away from our busy, overworked lives – and we'll see their light and be reminded that we're not alone and that somehow, everything will be okay if we can just close our eyes and fall asleep and wake with the rising sun of a brand new day.

And no matter where we live – the city, the suburbs, a small house or a big one – the same beautiful sky hovers over all of us each night like a warm blanket, reminding us we're not alone and that beauty is all around us.

Sometimes we just have to look up to see it.

That was the kind of love we had. A **timeless love** that didn't make us one person in and of the same, rather, it made us stronger in the things we loved and even happier together.

Love is not in material goods, rather, it's in a feeling that exists unconditionally between two people.

Honesty,
loyalty,
trust,
laughter,
unconditional love.
Share these with another
and you'll find
a richness no money can ever buy.

Despite a million odds,
we found our way back to each other.

Love is and of itself a risk. But in my heart, even in
    the midst of agony, I can tell you it's a risk worth
    taking.

HEARTBREAK

The absence of talking to you
deflates
all of my other actions.

You and me, we made a vow.
For better or worse;
I can't believe you let me down.
But the proof is in the way it hurts.
For months on end, I've had my doubts,
denying every tear.
I wish this would be over now,
but I know that I still need you here.

You say I'm crazy
'cause you don't think I know what you've done.
But when you call me Baby,
I know I'm not the only one.

You've been so unavailable,
now sadly, I know why.
Your heart is unobtainable
even though you still have mine.

I have loved you for so many years;
maybe I'm just not enough.
You've made me realize my deepest fear
by lying and tearing us apart.

MIRROR

This time it was more than your
wandering eyes that betrayed me.
This time you chose another to replace me.
We worked so hard together
to create this perfect life.
And just when everything fell into place,
you decided it wasn't enough.

That's when you said no one would ever love me.
You held me down.
You yelled and you screamed,
although *it shouldn't have been at me.*
Look in the mirror
and see who you've become.
Look in the mirror
at the monster you've created,
all in a vain attempt to hide your mistakes.

The sneaking around didn't stop.
I said *we're done* and then you lost it.
The lies and the pain,
they're too much to bear.
You're holding me in place to avoid your own guilt
and despair.
Let me go.
Speak the truth.
And get over yourself.

What you did was wrong,
but now that she's gone
you act like there's been
no harm.
I'm wounded and frozen.
Where have you gone?
You once were loving and devoted,
until she came along.

Please look in the mirror
and keep looking
until you see.

The mirror will show you everything.

I wasn't strong enough
to reciprocate the love that you had;
I wasn't brave enough to be vulnerable like that.
I wasn't ready to say those three words back.
I wasn't ready for a real love like that.
They say timing is everything
and clearly ours was off.
They say lots of things that I don't believe at all.
I'm sorry if I hurt you.
I'm sorry if that stung.
I'm sorry that I turned to run.
I hope that you have a good life now,
I hope that you found
the depth of love you deserve.
And I hope that you remember when...
once, you were my best friend.
I'm sorry I wasn't ready
for the love you had to give back then.

FOREVER

How long is forever?
I thought we'd spend it together
but life – or we – had plans of our own.
Plans to make it outside of the confines
    of our small town.
Plans to prove our worth to who – I don't know?
Were we supposed to be together?
How long is forever?
Whatever the answers are,
I guess we'll never know.

Old love is like a broken bone that's healed;
it still hurts sometimes when it rains.

You said your love for me was buried.
Real love never gets buried
and it doesn't bury the other person.

You did the very thing we swore we'd never do.
It's hard to believe there was a day
when we couldn't wait to say *I do*.
Nothing could stop us, not even a blizzard or two.

Oh, but look at this beautiful life we've built.
The little black mailbox bears our name.
The scuff marks on the walls are from our fingers,
and the sunflowers grow tall
because of the seeds we sowed.
How long do I wait?
Or is it too late?

We go to a concert
and you're eyeing the man on stage.
You think I don't know, but I do.
I stand by your side,
a smile on my face
as he falls for you
without even knowing your name.

You're gone more and more.
You think home life has become a bore.
I cook and I clean,
and you just grow mean.
As soon as he came into your life,
you stopped reaching your hand out for mine.

The story of us versus the world,
how can it end overnight?

I went to the cemetery today
to find the grave of a man who'd been brave,
and to say hello to an old flame.
I heard you whisper my name on the breeze.
The dogs barked and wagged their tails with knowing
and my eyes filled with tears.
It's been so many years.
Frozen in time you'll forever be,
you were always someone
who made people see.
My first love, my first crush.
My first so many things.
Even now, at your grave, you remind me
to feel,
to live,
to be fully present,
to embrace what we're given.
I can no longer see you,
but I know you're here.
You're in the rustling of the leaves
and in the growth of blossoming flowers.
You're in the rain and the river water.
I went to the cemetery today
It's been a long time
since your hand was in mine
but while visiting your stone,
I was reminded that I'll never be alone.

Our relationship should be a safe haven,
never a battlefield.
There's no room in love
for that kind of stress.
Love should be protective,
safe,
kind,
secure,
trustworthy, and stable.
Love should be the feeling of home;
like a soft blanket on a crisp fall night.
Love should always be what keeps us warm.

WAITING

It won't happen again, you say.
And I'm left waiting,
>   waiting,
>   waiting.

I'm sorry, you tell me.
And I'm left waiting,
>   waiting,
>   waiting.

This time it's different, you cry.
And I'm left waiting,
>   waiting,
>   waiting.

It wasn't my fault.
And I'm left waiting,
>   waiting,
>   waiting.

I didn't mean it.
And I'm left waiting,
>   waiting,
>   waiting.

You misunderstood.
And I'm left waiting,
>   waiting,
>   waiting.

Give me one more chance, you plead again.
And I'm left waiting,
     waiting,
          waiting.
It's been years of waiting and not much has changed.
Years of hoping.
Years of wanting.
And I'm left waiting,
     waiting
          waiting.
And I won't wait anymore.

EMPTY

I go to bed each night
starving
for your comfort,
wishing for your words,
hoping for connection.
But wishes don't
make changes,
people do.
And the person I've been waiting for is you.
I pick up the occasional crumbs you throw my way,
hoping they will fill me up to stay another day.
When will I finally realize
that this hunger – this starvation - is not okay?

Every time, you said
"But he's a *good man*,"
you told me to look beyond the dark cloak.
In silence I was left
to choke
on my muffled words
while yours echoed in my head.
Weary and confused,
I pushed ahead.
Until one day I said,
"*A good man* isn't one who puts you down,
he isn't quick with his hand or cruel with his words. He
isn't bitter with his tone."
"No," I told you. "A good man is kind.
He is compassionate and
full of good intentions.
He's someone who rules not with an iron fist,
but collaborates instead with an intelligent mind and a
beating heart.
He's someone who'll put your well-being
front and center, from the start.
He's someone whose words
wrap around you in warmth,
someone you don't make excuses for.
A good man he may want to be,
but what do his actions show?"
Despite what you tell me and yourself,
A good man is one who
never needs to be told he is so.

You tried to render me immobile,
but I kept moving anyway.
I took your hateful words
and although they hurt,
I piled them up,
tuned them upside-down
and made a crown.
You tried to stop me from rising,
but like a blade of grass
pushing through a break in the concrete,
I continued to grow.
And still, you tried to stop me.
But I kept pushing toward the sun.

EXPIRED LOVE

It's still strange when our eyes meet
    and your hand doesn't reach for mine.
It's still strange,
    the difference in the way you say my name.
It's still strange,
    all the memories we hold between us
    yet the vastly different lives we lead.
It's strange, all of it – what we call life.
We both expected to be one forever,
    only to be surprised by what came our way.
It's still so strange when you look my way
    and we don't move closer in some way.
It's still so strange that all we once had is gone,
    a mere story to tell
    with no one to listen.
It's still strange.

For your approval I lived
and you liked it that way.
Controlled by the invisible,
no apology did you ever say.
When I asked for your love
you said, of course.
But then quickly you turned the other way.
Where did you go?
Or were you ever really there?
The conditions on your so-called love
somehow held me in place
while you continued blowing plenty of hot air.
No more will I accept
the crumbs that you left.
No more will I say, *I love you, so it's okay*.
No more will I live for your approval
or be pulled by that manipulative thread.
I live now for a love I should have had all along.
A love for myself,
an unconditional one.
Approval for me, for who I truly am.
No more will I bow down to
your skits and scams.
I'll always love you
despite your lack of unconditional love for me,
but no longer can what we once had, still be.

You let me down
again and again.
Battered and bruised in my heart
I continued coming back
wishing you'd change,
wishing you'd see me for me,
wishing upon a star
that wasn't meant to be.
No worries,
I'm okay
despite all you did.
The bruises all healed in the end.
Without you I've learned to move on
so you can't let me down again.

I smiled until my cheeks bled
because I'd focused only on you instead.
No more will I do what I've been wrongly taught,
my love cannot and will not be bought.
I'm changing direction,
like it or not.

They pretended you did something wrong
to try and avoid feeling bad about
the things they've done
and said behind your back.

So far away I feel.
So delusional you are
in what you want to be real.
Whenever I've needed you most
you all became ghosts.
So far away I feel.
When my heart is broken it's a victory to you.
When my soul is happy
you turn the other cheek.
But you're supposed to be
    who I come to in times like these.
So far away I feel.

I roared in pain
wondering why.
You changed so quickly,
in the blink of an eye.
One flicker of attention
was all that it took.
Gone you went,
starting anew,
yet, begging me to somehow still help you.
My love was too deep to turn my cheek,
but I blistered with wounds
trying to save you.
I roared in pain
again and again
only to say *Enough!* in the end.

Your threats and lies
and bullying ways
won't stop me
from being who I am.
What you don't realize
is that your underhanded cruelty
shows your weakness
in more ways than one.
I pray for you, that one day
you'll see the sun
and that one day you'll find the strength and courage
to be the real you.
And in the meantime,
I'll keep being me
while you lose yourself inside the unnecessary armor
you pile on
always
still wishing the best for you.

An insult hidden behind a coy smile,
tell me, why has that become your style?
We used to laugh and play our days away
but you changed somewhere along the way.
Obsessed with one-upping, looks,
    and perceived fame
you were willing to throw all of the real things away.
I've waved to you, too many times now to count
hoping you'd come back to your authentic self.
But my arms have grown heavy and I must move on.
Still, I'll always hold onto a glimmer of hope
for you, for me, and for us to be
blissful and know that we're happy and content with
    who we're meant to be.

I cried on your shoulder last night
You listened to my sobs
but you did not act.
And that in itself was an act
that spoke loudly enough.

MULTIPLE FACES

You come and you go.
Who are you now?
My lover or my enemy?
I wish I knew somehow.

Her heart said yes
but her head said no.
She didn't know which way to go.

His ocean blue eyes held on to her
one last time
as he said a tearful goodbye.
The merry go 'round continues moving,
its forward motion
pausing for no one.
With his aging hand
he gripped tight to the golden pole
and whispered into the breeze,
"I hope one day we'll meet again."

You tell me we're "meant to be"
but am I strong or weak for staying?
You tell me "always and forever"
while I'm left wondering,
listlessly lingering for your affection.

She filled her life
with so much talk of death
that she forgot to live.

- Fear

All the lies you told,
now I know they were covering up
for why you had turned cold.
You turned your back on me when you met her.
In one swift second, life became a blur.
Now she's gone and you've come back.
Now you swear you never wanted anyone but me.
But what we had has turned dark.
It's too late for you to pretend to save the day.
We fell too far, my dear.
There are no more pieces to pick up.
What's done is done.
It's time to move on.

Desperate for the crumbs of your affection
I took you at your word,
even though I knew the truth.
Honestly, it all seemed so absurd.
Desperate for the crumbs of your affection
I couldn't stop longing for your false protection.

THE BLAME GAME

You blamed him.
You blamed her.
You blamed me.
You blamed everyone but yourself,
don't you see?
And in doing so, you lost me.

I reach out for you with my words
again and again
only to find you absent
when I'm ready to begin.

One little lie,
two little lies.
Suddenly, they multiply
surrounding me like fireflies.
Alluring they may seem
and hard to capture, they are.
What you don't see against the blinking lights
is that your quiet lies leave behind
a thousand scars.

Agitation is a feeling that says many things.
It whispers the truth and clips our **wings**.
It tries to tell us with a feeling
that to which we often turn a deaf ear.
The reason it arises is because of our own fear.
Fear of what we know is **true**,
but for one reason or another don't want to accept.
The secret is that the feeling will only subside
when our heart and head align.

He found me on a warm summer day.
Despite what peering eyes may have thought,
he had not come to play.
Instead, he came to hold my hand.
Two mere strangers;
    one entering a new and distant land.
He faded quickly, once he knew he was safe.
It broke my heart that he'd come to know love, much
    too late.

How can I open my heart to you after
you were the one who shattered it?
You tell me to forget the bad,
to remember the good,
and move on...just like that.
What you don't realize is that the body remembers –
and that includes the heart.
And what it recalls is too harsh for the light of day,
too much to risk
when something still feels so amiss.
And despite how I've loved you, deeply and fully,
our lips can no longer linger to meet in a kiss.

A flat apology doesn't make it better.
Only a pure and well-intentioned heart
has the power to do that.

I love you.
You broke my heart in two.
I love you.
You broke my heart in two.
Tell me,
Where do we go?
Is love enough?
Or, is it time to let go?

I lay by your side, night after night.
Your skin touches mine,
but closeness evades me.
For, try as I may,
I cannot open up to the one who betrayed me.

Love is a tricky thing.
You can't hold it in your hands.
Nor can you bottle it up.
And if one of two takes it for granted
what once was magic
will
      slip
         away.

It burns,
it stings;
the sharp tears
and the echoing pain.
What do you do
when your heart is broken in two?

A rogue tear falls,
staining my porcelain face,
leaving a lasting crevice in its place.
A fissure of *Before and After* has been made,
I see it in my reflection now,
day after day.

I toss and turn
and long for sleep
and when it comes,
seldom as it does,
I wake,
covered in soft drips of saltwater
manufactured by a broken heart.
I stare
at the wall
and wonder why.
I close my eyes and ponder
how I'll tell you I love you,
despite the fact that to what once was Us,
I say goodbye.
I fear these tears
will forever stay in my eyes.

Her words said, *"I'm done,"*
but her tone said, *"I still love you."*
It was a battle of mind versus heart
and even she didn't know
which would win in **The End**.

I love you so much,
but something more than love
is needed to save us now.

What has been done has been done
and what has been said has been said.
None of it can be erased
or changed.
It is written into history,
weaved intricately into the fabric of
Our Story, forever.

I've tried again and again to help you,
to pull the darkness out of you,
only to feel like a magician
pulling at an infinite silk,
because there is no end.

You did the worst thing you could do;
you broke my heart in two.
Then, I tell you I need you.
You tell me I'm too needy now.
But I need you to hold me, somehow.
I need you to hold me tight and
be the one to tell me
everything's going to be alright.

I need you to take my hand,
I need you to help make our plans.
I need you so I can breathe again,
but you don't want me to be that way.
You don't want me to need anything.

You want me to forget it all.
You want me to pretend we didn't fall.
You want to laugh and dance like it didn't matter.
While I'm stuck trying to silence
all of the chatter.

I need you in every way, but you say
my neediness
is driving you away.
Is real love supposed to hold you down?
Because now you're telling me to
bow my head
to the ground.

Is real love supposed to hurt like this?
My heart aches at what's missing now
when we kiss.

Once addicted to another's alluring eyes,
you try your best
to comfort me with lies.
You did the worst thing you could do;
you broke my heart in two.
Then, I told you I needed you.

But even when you hold my hand
I'm left wondering...
I'm left needing...
I'm left, like a puddle on the floor...

You want me back, now that she's gone
but I need you
and you tell me
that's what's wrong.

REGRET

Life goes by so fast,
keep your promises while you still can.
If you know she's wishing for that one thing,
give it to her now before it fills you with
the heartache
of a forever regret.
Because once she's gone, she's gone.
And in the ground, you can't feel her now.
Although you see your name carved
forever beside hers,
yours is still an empty dash.

You can't make up for what you lacked.
You can't take those harsh words back
and you can't hold her in your arms
the way she ached for you to do for so long.
We're all on a merry go 'round called life,
but we don't get to live it twice.
No, we don't get to live it twice.
We get one time around
and we better make it count.

You spend your nights in front of the screen
instead of making memories.
She looks at you longingly
and you pretend not to notice
because you don't think you have to.
But these moments are so fleeting.
And the minutes are ticking.

Your children are all grown
with families of their own.
The house is quiet with just the two of you.
You fill the silence
between the walls
with whatever distractions you can find
but not with
the one thing
you know she's looking for.

And then the pain comes
and it's over before you know it.
The pain that took her away
from this beautiful life
the two of you made.
As she breathed her last breath,
you held her soft hand with so much regret.
And now she's gone.
It's like trying to hold water in your hands.
You can't get that time back.
The minutes are always ticking.

I'm learning that soulmates are real,
but they're not always meant to be together.
To have that privilege,
both people have to be all in,
they have to make the right choices, always.

There are fleeting moments when you look at me in
the daylight and tell me with your eyes that you're
sorry. I feel it and I hear your voice echo through
the hollows of my aching body. It confuses me,
the back and forth, from good to bad.

Although you won't tell me in words,
I know your pain.
Although your actions are angry,
I know your pain.
Although your spine is straight and your chin is high,
I know your pain.
Although you smile, your eyes still tell the truth;
I know your pain.
Although you often scowl, fearful of your shadow,
I know your pain.
And although I know,
I promise to keep your secret
and to sit with you any time you need to.
And when you're ready to put into words
the pain that anchors you,
I'll be here to listen
and I'll be here to hold you.
I know your pain
because **You and I are one in the same.**
I can see and feel all the things
you do not know how to say.
I know you're scared,
but you no longer need to be
because now you are safe, and you can just be.

WHAT YOU SAY VS WHAT YOU DO

Walks to the park and Sunday morning brunch.
He loved her always,
but it was never enough.
The bottle and the pills won every time
even when he let himself look into her big brown
eyes.
His little girl.
His flesh and blood.
She was his everything,
yet he couldn't give the bottle up.

"It'll be different this time," he'd say.
"All the bad has gone away.
It'll be different this time, I promise.
Just watch and I'll be honest."

Missing again, she'd find him
slumped over in the corner of another dive bar.
He'd need a ride from his little girl
who'd grown up overnight.
His little girl.
His flesh and blood.
She was his everything,
yet he couldn't give up the bottle up.

Another stint behind bars, another plea for help.
Another broken promise,
oh well.
But then he looks into her big brown eyes
wishing he could stop the lies.
Wishing he could be a better man.
His little girl.
His flesh and blood.
She was his everything,
yet he couldn't give the bottle up.

FALLING

I shattered into a million pieces
   and you
   watched them fall to the ground.
Afterward, you walked away, again.

That's the story of a broken heart.
That's the story of an extinguished flame.

All it took was just one look
   and you left me for her.
You swore it wasn't love
   but the stain on your skin told the truth.
   You pushed aside what we had
   for rejuvenated youth.

Secret dates and late-night talks,
   your mind was addicted to the new.
A high,
   a rush,
   it's what you sought
   no matter the cost.
You wanted what you wanted,
even though you knew.

Always gone, hiding secrets,
    you wanted her, and she wanted you.
But after seventeen years, I still loved you.
What did she have that I didn't?
I guess I'll never know.

I can't make you love me,
    and I can't stop wondering why.
What was once yellow and bright
    has now turned charcoal gray.
And then,
    here comes the kicker,
    when she moved away,
    suddenly,
        you wanted me back.
Only then, you realized that we'd shattered into a
million pieces.

Those nights you left me lying alone in bed
while you hid in the dark
with another
wrapped tightly in your arms -
that's when the light left my eyes
and trust drained painfully from my veins.

I still wanted you back.
I still felt I needed you
but you were gone.
You were so far gone.

And there I was,
my head on the pillow
beside an empty space.
There I was,
wondering what I'd done to make you run.
There I was, no longer who I once knew
holding on to what I could of my memories
with you.

You became a *we* with someone other than me,
something you swore
you'd never do.
You became a totally different version of you.

Where'd you go, my love?
Why'd you up and leave?
Where'd you go, my love?
Why'd you deceive me?

The not knowing is part of the adventure,
but it can also be madness.

The waiting...
the endless waiting
creates an endless ebb and flow
of hope and worry.
And so I keep waiting,
hoping for hope
and hoping there will be
no more waiting.

I've never been a praying woman,
but I've fallen to my knees a lot lately,
hoping the angels might hear me
and bestow upon me the strength necessary
to get through.

WE LOST A BEAT

Among the chaos
we lost a part of Us.
Yet, we didn't give up.
Others told us, "*Move on.*"
Others told us, "*It's time.*"
But all the while
I still longed for your hand in mine.

We lost a beat.
It went on too long.
Remember when we sang the same song?
Surrounded by bullies,
surrounded by lies,
we lost a beat
and I'd feared what had once been ours was gone.

We struggled.
I cried.
We argued.
You moved.
We lost a beat.

That muzzle you wore
opened a wrong door.
I went this way and that
    through the labyrinth you'd made
only to wonder whose hands were at your aid.

We lost a beat.
Then finally, we knew
that the truth and our words would
make us anew.

Honesty and loyalty rolled in from the fog.
Rise is what we did from the ashes of that rotten log.

Once upon a time, we lost a beat
but we didn't let it become our defeat.
Instead we stood up on our bare feet,
we took the care and the time
to make ourselves complete.
And with that becoming, we sang once again.
My hand fell back into yours,
forward we swam.

We lost a beat, once, years ago.

COURAGE
&
RESILIENCE

I've been waiting patiently for you to stop being
complacent and start living.

Y
O
U
R
    L
    I
    F
    E

The raven rising
they did not see.
That raven is me.

What is your truth?
What is it you want to say, but haven't?

You are a magnificent being,
full of creation
and the immense ability
    to do great things for this world.
Believe.

The wave overtook me,
while everyone scattered.
Destitute and alone,
scared at first,
worry set in.
But then I realized the truth,
and that's when I rose
TALLER and STRONGER than I was before.
Suddenly awake,
I hadn't been knocked down.
I'd been shown the truth
letting it wash over me.
And with that truth I now **RISE.**
And with that rising I **thrive.**
And with that thriving **I KNOW.**
And with that knowing **I am.**
And with that, **I AM whole.**
I am everything that is **magic.**
I am uniquely and decidedly **ME**.

I wake to the morning light
only to still be
heavily veiled
by the darkness of night.

That mask
you wear
isn't yours to bear.
No,
it was meant for the one
who placed it there.

You speak ill of me
for all of the things
within yourself
you refuse to see.

"Do as I say!" he shouted at me.
"And one day I'll make you
old and bitter,
just like me."

All this big talk
and I can't find
the action.

Trapped
in a box
trying to outrun
the flame.
Blinded by it all,
fooled by love.
All while sitting across
from you
in smiles.
I think
I can
go on like this
for miles and miles.

**"Run wild
and be free, little one," she said.
"Away from the heavy chains
that have always kept me."**

PRETENDING
your life
is a certain way
doesn't make it so.
No,
Instead it strangles you
and prevents you from truly growing.

Listen
carefully
to my words,
look into my eyes.
Can you see
the pain
in my heart?

*"You have something
great that others don't,"* he said,
before turning to look
the other way.

I ran in circles
for years
trying to save you,
only to find
in the end,
there was never
anything new.

When I look
at you
I remember
the significance
of sweet December.

She hid
his secret
for years.
What she didn't realize
is that it would all
REAPPEAR.

And then,
one night
you told me,
and suddenly
it all made sense.
I could finally see
the real you
who'd been hiding
behind all of the mess.

The thick forest envelopes me
in its leafy branches,
taking me in,
sheltering me from the bitter tones of others
and restoring me,
again and again
to all that I am meant to be.
The trees offer me the protection that I seek,
reminding me that all hope is not lost
because there is a fire burning inside of me
that is capable of warming humanity
if only I can find the **resilience and strength**
to stand tall and walk outside of their branches.

The wind whispered to me:
find yourself
and be that.

I'm proud of you, for being you.
I'm proud of you, remember that.

Hold on to my hand
no matter
where you go.
Darling dear,
don't let them
make you
part of
their show.

You may dismiss her,
deeming her small.
But you're in for a
surprise!
because a raven
sees all.

PICTURE IT

Picture yourself at age five.
What would you say to that
young, innocent, wide-eyed child?
If given the chance,
what would you tell that smaller version of yourself?
Is there something you could say
that would help you today?
Something that would make it all okay?
Whatever it is, say it loud.
Tell yourself what you needed to hear then,
because you still need it now.

Those golden shackles you wear
   won't get you anywhere.
Pretty as they may be,
   their only purpose is the illusion of comfort,
   but at what cost?
Is the illusion worth the sacrifice?
If your answer is Yes,
I'm quite sure you're lost.
If you want to know what true emancipation is,
dare to take off those shackles and begin to swim.
Sure, it's scary
   and nothing is certain,
   but wouldn't you rather live life by your own rules
   than be led by the current?
Wouldn't you rather taste freedom
   than succumb to false certainty?
Wouldn't you rather lay your wrists bare,
   than to be decorated with those
   sparkly golden shackles
   that were only designed to keep you there?

I may look
meek
and innocent
yet I am as fierce
and mighty
as a storm
you don't see coming.

"Please," she yelled.
"Come back to me."
But his face,
she never actually did see.

"I love him,"* she yelled
And I questioned,
"More than yourself?"

They took you away,
dabbled you in fame.
I longed for your kiss
and walked alone
through the flames.
From the ashes
we rose
on our tippy-toes,
escaping the fire
that scorched our clothes.
We stood hand in hand
and took back our land.
Stronger than them,
T-O-G-E-T-H-E-R
we still stand.

All of the elements
of Mother Nature –
lions hunting gazelle in the prairie,
elephant herds welcoming new calves
and slowing their pace to
accommodate,
birds flocking together
to fend off their prey –
all of Her elements are inside
every woman –
fierce,
strong,
loyal,
intelligent,
protective,
bearing new life…
A female's instinct is a force
never to be messed with.
Like Mother Nature,
if you steal from Her,
abuse Her,
or take Her for granted,
Her wrath of retaliation
may not always be swift,
but it will certainly be
significant and lasting –
changing the natural course of things
forever.
For every element of Mother Nature
is also in the possession of every woman.

Fake names,
phony smiles,
it was all just a game.
You traveled for miles
to make me insane.
Too bad for you,
I saw right through it all.
The evil charade
you all tried to play.
Only,
I called you out
with a single shout.
And off you ran
to distant lands,
thinking you were safe
from the karma
you'd already set in motion.
Thinking you were invincible
only to find, in the end,
you were mortal.

You tried
your best
to take me down.
And when
I knew,
you suddenly
left town.
Running
will only
get you so far.
Karma, you see
will stick
to your precious
black wings
like tar.

Bullies who are trying
to scare you
are the ones
who are scared themselves.

New skin
forms over
old scars
leaving even
the best of us
to wonder
WHO
we really are.

You hunted me,
innocent prey.
Now you're in the zoo;
time to let the lions come out to play.

"Come with me," she said.
"It will be all right."
"Trust me," I replied.
"And we'll make it through the night."

"Hear me roar!" Ego said.

And Confidence replied with silence.

"Can't you hear me?" Ego asked.

"Answer me now!" Ego continued.

But Confidence continued standing still and quiet.

Ego stomped one foot and then the other.

"Is this a game?" Ego shouted.

"Because, you should know, I win all games," Ego promised.

And still, Confidence only smiled.

"I'm bigger than you! And stronger, too!"

Ego grew angrier with each new word.

"I once captured an entire herd of elephants," Ego lied.

But it was only by silence that his empty words were denied.

"Hey you, over there, listen to me!"

But in response, Confidence simply let Ego be.

On and on the cycle went.

Until one day, it seemed Ego might relent.

"Hear me roar!" Ego tried yelling once more.

Only, this time Ego's voice fell flat.

"Why won't you respond to me?" Ego pleaded.

Clearing her throat, Confidence calmly spoke,

"Because there's never a need to give attention to that kind of greed."

She runs just like her;
fast and free.
And she sounds just like him;
A good kind of wild, and always full of glee.
Yet her own person she'll become –
determined and **unique.**

When she walked into a room,
the energy shifted.
Lights became brighter
and the darkness faded into oblivion.

*When you don't know what to
believe in,
believe in yourself.
Believe.
Believe that even in the darkness,
spots of light will show themselves.*

START DIGGING

Whatever that dream is that you've buried deep
    inside of you,
it's time to unbury it.
It's time to stop ignoring it.
It's time to stop fearing it.
It's time to stop and let it begin to grow, instead of
    letting it go.
Whatever that dream is you've buried deep inside of
    you,
it's time to start digging and let the sunshine in.

A dream doesn't have to be big to be a dream.
A dream is what brings happiness and contentment.
It's a well lived life.
A dream isn't one big moment of triumph
and it isn't fame or riches or appearances.
A dream is what already exists inside of you.
It's a gift you need to give yourself
one day after the next,
because a life without a dream
and without gratitude
will quickly fill with regrets.

Have whatever material possessions you must,
have whatever career you choose.
Have whatever house you wish to call a home.
But never forget,
it's what you have inside of you that's real.

I want you to learn how to embrace the life you have,
the one you've been given, even if you think it
looks different than the lives of others. It's yours.

I only have to be,
and by being,
I AM ENOUGH.

THE ACCIDENTAL REBEL

My soul is broken.
My heart, wounded.
My brows, knitted.
The parenthesis around my mouth, deepened.
The half-moons beneath my eyes, purpled.
For days and months,
for years and decades,
I've allowed you to hurt me with your daggered
    words.
I've allowed you to bludgeon me with passive
    aggressiveness
and I've allowed you to cut me with your secrets and
    half-truths.
One day, I looked in the mirror
and realized, nothing changes unless I do.
And so, I'm changing
here and now.
I won't allow your ever-sharpening blade to strike me
    again.
You've placed me on the outside
and for so long it hurt,
but now I see the truth.
No longer are my glasses dappled by your fog.
If you think I'm a rebel,
let me be.
I am what I am
and you can no longer hurt me
because I am *finally free*.

He knew if he wanted to do big things with his life, he couldn't let the small things or the small-minded people get him down.

A label of position doesn't make your life "good" or "bad." You make it what you want by the choices you make and the actions you take.

Let the art of creation be a warm blanket that wraps
  around you in comfort.

We all make sacrifices, whether we go after what we
  want or whether we settle with our lives.
  Make your sacrifices count.

People think they know everything about everyone,
  when the truth is, they know nothing at all.

Moments matter,
  regardless of how fleeting they may be.
They matter and they stay with us,
  leaving impressions on our souls for a lifetime.

I want my daughters to have a mother who tells
    them they can be anything they want to be and
    love anyone they want to love, so long as they are
    happy.

Manners are a currency indulged by
grateful souls.
And grateful souls shall be filled with
endless gold.

People are quick to judge, so quick to make an assessment of someone, even when they have so little information. They have no idea what's truly going on below the surface. They only see the exterior.

The smiles.

The new outfits.

The image that's presented to the world.

Hardly ever do people take the time to see anything more. They're too busy caught up in thoughts of how others might have it easier than them. But the truth is, it's hard for all of us. We all have our battles to face in life. And our job isn't to judge others, it's to support them and it's to help them up when they fall down. It's to **be kind** and **compassionate**, even when we ourselves are going through a tough time. Our job as humans is to **make the world a warmer, better place,** not a colder one.

I'm at a crossroad,
    unsure of which way to turn.
Too many perceived friends have become enemies
    and lovers have become confusions –
    all of it swirling in a tornado,
    spitting me out at a crossroad.
I look to my left.
I look to my right.
I look up ahead and behind.
Which way do I go next?
And what will I find?
Only I can decide,
    and to do that I must step in a direction
    without the influence of others.
I must trust my gut.
Hold my chin high.
And be ready to see what lies ahead.

Too sensitive, he said
telling me I live too much in my heart and head.
Where else should I live? I wondered.
Who else should I be? I worried.
Until I realized I was being misled.
For life is meant to be lived
and to live is to listen to your own soul,
to come alive with all the things that
make it your own.
Sensitive I may be,
but I will no longer apologize
because I now live a life where I am free.

Everything changes
yet our bodies forever remember,
whispering truths to us although we're not always
aware.
Telling us what it knows
in hopes of helping us somehow.
But so often we don't pause to listen.
Illusionary changes take place
while history repeats,
begging us to hear what it has to say.
Telling us it has the answers to help us make
everything okay.

You think she doesn't know.

She Knows.

You think I don't know.

I Know.

You think they don't know.

They Know.

Everyone Knows.

What you've done, you can't undo.

Instead, it will stick to its doer like glue.

As careful as you thought you may have been,

people make mistakes now and then.

Watch as she rises with what *She Knows*.

It will surely keep you on the tip of your toes.

The invisible scars are often
the most painful wounds of all.

Dear Self,

It is never okay for anyone to threaten you.
It is never okay for anyone to strike you.
It is never okay to be shoved into walls.
It is never okay to be cheated on.
It is never okay to be the recipient of lies.
You deserve respect,
unconditional love,
kindness,
compassion,
non-violence,
open communication,
trust,
and honesty.
You deserve all the good things that life can be.

I'm mesmerized by nature. Humans build paved roadways, sidewalks, and all types of infrastructure. And still, grass finds a way to grow through the cracks. Nature is always trying to come back, to make things the way they should be. The world craves balance. The earth wants all living beings to thrive, not merely a few. Birds spend their lives eating worms and ants, but when the bird dies, ants and worms eat it. The balance of power constantly shifts to allow the world to thrive.

Sometimes I wonder, aren't we all just playing a part? Aren't we all hiding behind masks, always quietly fearful our truths will be seen?

HEALING THE WOUND

I spend my life
fixing in others,
what is broken in me.

You dared to cast false smiles my way,
all while hiding your plan.
You dared to try and destroy what wasn't yours
all while calling it play.
You gave your life to the dark
and tried to overtake the light.
But what you failed to realize was that
light will always win.
The stars and the moon brighten the inky night sky
and every morning for all of time,
when the glowing moon rests,
his faithful companion shines even brighter,
assuring us all again and again
    that light will always win.

They tried to burn us, to turn us into ashes.
They didn't know we were the fire.
We can burn forever with their matches.

What's done is done. Moments are forever, never
    able to be changed. No amount of *"I'm Sorrys"* or
    "I wish I would haves" will change a moment once
    it's taken place.

The choices we make will ultimately
    determine the life we get.

She wished she could magically heal his wounds,
    imagining that her touch could somehow undo the
    past and the pain that came with it.

It's odd how we remember certain moments in life; certain lines people said. And the way they echo back to us later in life, providing a sense of direction, perhaps when we need it most. We never know how **our words** might impact someone else throughout *their* lifetime.

How lucky I am to be Enough.

Enough as a woman.

Enough without children.

Enough with children.

Enough by working in the home.

Enough by working outside of the home.

Enough to love at free will.

Enough to have an opinion and let it be heard.

Enough to enjoy a good book.

Enough to decide my own finances.

Enough to laugh when it strikes me to do so.

Enough to wear a dress or to wear pants.

Enough to stand tall, despite those who try to
   oppress.

Enough to make my own choices with my body.

Enough to know when I've had enough.

Enough to be brave and strong,
   and to be simultaneously compassionate and kind.

How lucky I am to be Enough
   exactly as I am.

There are so many opposing words that, upon closer inspection, contain the same number of letters.

Negative and *Positive* each have eight letters.

Evil and *live* each have four.

How many more can you name?

Let's transform the *negatives* into *positives* and choose the better side of life.

YOU TRIED

You tried to tell her she wasn't enough.
You tried to put poison in her blood.
You tried to manipulate and control
   under the guise of something good.
You think you're invincible,
   you think no one knows.
You all hide behind masks
   while you try to create a show.
Hide though you try
   behind those fleeting smiles –
   time is up.
You can't run any more miles.
While the bullied gains justice
   and stands tall,
   the bullies see who wasn't enough after all.
Look in the mirror
   as you recite those hurtful words you said;
   the words you used to make others small.
Stare hard at your reflection
   as the words come back to you;
   each and every one is sure to infiltrate you.
As in all stories,
   this also holds true:
   what you did wrong,
   will come back to you.

THANK YOU

Battered and bruised,
    what will I do?
I will heal these wounds,
stand up and say, "Thank You."
Thank You to the ones who tried to step on me.
Thank You to those who doubted me.
Thank You for showing me who I never want to be.
Thank You for pushing me to the path that was
    meant for me.
Battered and bruised,
    what will I do?
I will heal these wounds,
    stand up and with a smile, say,
        "Thank You."

What you are doing to another,
    will come back 'round to you.

When I am who I am
and not who you are,
when you are who you are
and not who I am
then, and only then,
we will both stand tall
and embrace the wonders of us all.

We all have stones thrown at us at one time or
    another. Don't let yours sink you. Instead, use
    those stones to build a beautiful home with a
    foundation that keeps you safe, where joy is
    endless, where love is unconditional, and where
    possibilities are infinite.

You can heal from those deep, buried wounds
   inside of you;
   the ones you don't want anyone to see.
You can heal
   if you pause
   if you acknowledge
   if you accept
   and if you let yourself be.
I promise **you can heal** from these wounds
   inside of you.

"I'm Sorry." I want to say this to you for all the
    people who should have and never did.
I'm Sorry.
I'm Sorry.
I'm Sorry.
I'm Sorry.
I'm Sorry.
I'm Sorry.
I'm Sorry.
I'm Sorry.
I'm Sorry.
I'm Sorry.
I'm Sorry.
I'm Sorry.
I'm Sorry.
I'm Sorry.
I'm so incredibly sorry.

WHO?

Who did this to me?
The wrinkles around my eyes.
The dots on my skin.
The scar on my foot,
    and these hands, look at them,
    shriveled and ripe.
The figure looking back at me in the mirror
    is hardly mine.

Who did this to me? I ask again.
Only to realize the answer is staring back at me; it's
    life.
I've lived; I am living.
I did this, not out of harm, but from love.
The wrinkles are from smiling – at our wedding and
    other celebrations,
    from falling in love, and from the birth of new little
    ones.
The dots on my arms are from gardening beneath the
    warm glow of the sun.
I love my life so much that I've dared to live.
I did this; all of it.
And with this realization,
I am no longer ashamed of the lines on my skin.
Instead, I will celebrate them.
Because I've lived; I'm living.
And really, what's more beautiful
    than a life well-lived?

Big and little
side by side.
You took me to the bookstore
and opened my eyes.
To possibilities,
to ideas,
to wonder and awe,
to dreams,
to goals,
to a moment of "ah-ha."

Time keeps marching forward even if you stand still and beg it to stop. Time, he'd learned, stops for nothing and no one.

CATCH ME

I remember walking out onto the diving board
desperate to be brave.
You watched as your little girl
decided it was time to take the jump that day.
You reached your hands up to me
and I closed my eyes
and took the leap
into the deep blue water below,
where you were waiting for me.

And just like that, I knew
you'd catch me when I needed you.
Nothing's changed since that day
except the length of my legs
and the wisdom that lines your face.
Just like that, I knew.

You told me to hold my chin high
when I didn't make the team.
You let me know that my worth
was more than that
and that
you'd always love me.

And then one day,

when my heart breaks,

I'm desperate to be brave, like the diving board day.

I crumble in fear, unable to reason.

You reach your arms around me

and tell me to hold on tight.

You catch me again,

and again,

and again.

You catch me every time.

Hold your chin high, little butterfly. Dance to the beat that's marching inside of your soul. Laugh at yourself. Love yourself. And take flight, because you can. Because you've worked hard for this. Because you want to live your best life, and when you grow wings, it's such a thrill to fly.

You are enough exactly as you are.
A million times enough.
Please remember this.

I have finally figured out who I am and what I want in life and it's the greatest freedom a person could ever dream of finding.

We're all given this superpower, the power of choice, and although we can't always control what circumstances we're placed in, we can choose our reactions.

...what is supposed to be doesn't matter to me. What matters to me, is what actually is.

The rocks along the coast are
perfectly imperfect
like all of us.
They've endured years upon years of hardships,
of waves crashing relentlessly against them.
And yet, they still stand firm and strong,
perfectly imperfect.

Your energy speaks louder
than your words ever will.
I hear you.
Do you hear yourself?

She buried her face into her hands,
only to reemerge a changed woman.

There once was a little girl and everyone told her NO.
When she grew up, it was more of the same.
So, one day, instead of being crushed beneath the
    weight of other's opinions and commands,
    she told herself YES.
And that was the start of everything beautiful.

...**despite my fears,** I did what I knew in my heart was right. I lived the life I wanted to, the life that was waiting for me if I was **brave** enough to pursue it. I'm **proud** that I was **courageous** in the face of fear. And I want you to be brave, too. I want you to learn how to embrace the life you have, the one you've been given, even if it looks different from the lives of others. Always remember it is uniquely yours.

She sighed
as she stared at her reflection
knowing that an act that would enable
internal liberation
lay patiently waiting
for her to rise
to **the woman
she was born to be**.

It is a compelling story of love,
passion,
compassion,
and redemption.

Y
O
U
R

L
I
F
E

When you're old...
I want you to know you lived a happy life.
I want you to say you would do it all the same way if you had the chance to live your life again.

As sure as the flower blooms,

so too, will I.

THANK YOU!

Words and stories have inspired me from my earliest days. Their power is incredible. They bring us strength in the most difficult of times. They enable us to extend joy, evoke positive change, inform, and inspire. How amazing is it that with twenty-six letters, we're given the ability to create limitless magic in limitless forms?

The words of many: *Maya Angelou, Jane Goodall, Henry David Thoreau, and E.B. White* run through me. They echo through my mind each day, words from another time and in some cases, another place, that provide me strength, inspiration, and passion. Even in our modern, overworked, overstressed world, words still touch our hearts. They often leave us pausing to ponder how the words themselves specifically transfer to us in our current state of being.

Thank you for reading *Love & Courage*. I hope you've enjoyed it and I hope you'll revisit it time and again throughout your life. Each time, the meaning of the words may change for you. Each time, you may find something new hidden between the spaces, waiting there to help you heal or to help you open your heart once again. I believe there is both connection and power in words and it is my hope that both will find you throughout the pages of this book.

Sincerely,

S.L. Ritz

NOTE: If you enjoyed this book, please be sure to leave an online review to help other readers find the book. Thank you for your support!

FICTION NOVELS BY RITZ

The Lost Years
Goodbye, Hello
All the Little Choices
Intriguing Illusions
Sixty Seconds of Love
The Perfect Divorce
Inconceivable Lives
The Obsession
Keeping Up Appearances

Find more: *staceyritzbooks.com*

MOTIVATIONAL BOOKS BY RITZ

Pursuing Greatness: Strategies to Gain a Mental Edge in Sports and Life
Be Awesome: How to Live Your Best Life

Learn more: *staceyritzbooks.com*

ANIMAL WELFARE BOOKS BY RITZ

Covered in Pet Fur: How to Start an Animal Rescue,
the Right Way
Pawsitive Connection: Heartwarming Stories
Cat Connection: Heartwarming Rescue Tales
Fun(d)raising: 150 Money Making Ideas
Letters from Cats: Hilarious & Heartfelt Notes
Not Your Average Grandma: The Story of a Little
Senior Rescue Dog with Big Life Lessons

Find more: *advocates4animals.com*

POETRY BY RITZ

Love & Courage

Learn more: *staceyritzbooks.com/poetry*